Bible Dictionary
A first reference book

By Etta Wilson and Sally Lloyd Jones
Illustrated by Steven D. Schindler

STANDARD
PUBLISHING

Aa

Abba

The word **abba** is a child's word for father, like "daddy." Jesus **taught** us to call God **abba**.

afraid

When you are **afraid**, you are scared. David wasn't **afraid** of Goliath, even though Goliath was much bigger and **stronger** than he.

alive

Anything living is **alive**. Plants and animals are **alive**. Jesus made a little girl **alive** again.

altar

An **altar** is a special place to **worship** God. An **altar** is like a table and people gave **sacrifices** on it. Noah built an **altar** after the **flood**.

amen

People say **amen** at the end of a **prayer**. When you say **amen**, you are saying, "That's right!" or, "Yes, I agree!"

angel

An **angel** is a **heavenly** messenger sent by God. God sent the **angel** Gabriel to tell Mary that she would be the mother of Jesus.

angry

If you are **angry**, you are mad or unhappy with someone. The **Bible** says we shouldn't go to bed when we're **angry**.

anoint

If you **anoint** someone, you pour oil or **perfume** on them. **Anointing** people shows they are special. Samuel **anointed** David to be **king**.

apostle

An **apostle** is a special **helper**. Jesus **chose** twelve of his **disciples** to be his **apostles**. The **apostles** told everyone they met about Jesus.

appear

When someone **appears**, you suddenly see them but you don't see where they come from. A man **appeared** in the middle of the burning **furnace** with Daniel's **friends**.

ark

An **ark** is a chest or a box.
1. Noah built a huge **ark** to carry the animals when God sent the **flood**. Noah's **ark** was a boat.

2. The **ark** of the **covenant** was a special **gold**-covered box. The **ark** held the **Ten Commandments**.

armor

Armor is a suit of metal that **soldiers** wore. **Armor** kept them safe in **battle**.

army

A large group of **soldiers** is called an **army**.

Bb

Baal

Baal was a made-up god that some people in **Bible** times **worshiped** instead of God. God sent Elijah to show everyone that **Baal** was not God.

baby

A **baby** is a very young boy or girl. You used to be a **baby**. God became a **baby** and lived on earth. His name was Jesus.

baptize

When John **baptized** Jesus, he put Jesus under the water for a moment and then raised him up.

basket

A **basket** is like a bag made of grass or **reeds**. Moses' mother hid him in a **basket** that floated on the water.

battle

A **battle** is a fight between **enemies**. God's people had many **battles** with the **Philistines**.

bear

A **bear** is a big wild animal. It has thick fur and strong claws. David killed a **bear** while looking after his **sheep**.

beggar

A **beggar** is someone who is poor and gets **help** by asking strangers for **gifts**. Jesus made a **blind beggar** see.

believe

When you **believe** something, you **know** it is **true** or real. **Christians believe** that the **Bible** is true.

betray

You **betray** someone when you quit being their **friend**. You do something to hurt them instead. Judas **betrayed** Jesus to his **enemies**.

Bible

The **Bible** is a group of books. The **Bible** tells us the story of God and how he **loves** us.

blessing

A **blessing** is something good from God. When you **bless** someone, you are saying you want God to give what is best for them.

blind

A **blind** person is someone whose eyes don't work. If you are **blind**, you cannot see. Jesus made **blind** people see.

blood

Blood is the red stuff you see when you cut yourself. God turned all the water in Egypt into **blood** so that the **Egyptians** would **free** his people.

body

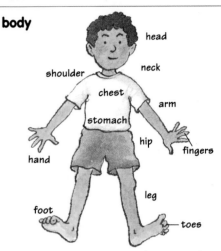

Your **body** is every part of you. God made your **body**.

bread

Bread is a food made from flour and **yeast**. Jesus fed over 5,000 people with just five loaves of **bread** and two small **fish**!

brother

A **brother** is a boy who is in your **family**. **Christians** are all **brothers** and sisters in God's family.

bury

When you **bury** something, you hide it in the ground to keep it safe. Jesus told a story of a man who **found** a treasure **buried** in a field.

camel

A **camel** is an animal that lives in the **desert**. **Camels** have one or two humps on their backs. In **Bible** times people traveled on **camels**.

cave

A **cave** is a hollow place, like a room, in the side of a hill or mountain. David hid from his **enemies** in a **cave**.

centurion

A **centurion** was a **Roman army** officer in charge of 100 **soldiers**.

chains

A **chain** is a string of metal loops hooked together. Peter was tied with **chains** for telling people about Jesus. God sent an **angel** to break the **chains**.

chariot

A **chariot** is a fast cart with two wheels that is pulled by horses. **Pharaoh** sent his **soldiers** in **chariots** to chase after Moses and God's people.

choose

If you **choose** something, you pick it out from everything else. God **chose** Abraham and his **descendants** to be his special people.

Christ — see **Messiah**

Christian

Anyone who **believes** and **obeys** Jesus is called a **Christian**. The **disciples** were **first** called **Christians** at Antioch.

church

A **church** is a group of **Christians** who meet together to **worship** God. The building where the **church** meets is sometimes also called a **church**.

city

A **city** is a place where people live that is larger than a **town**. Joshua fought the **battle** of Jericho and the walls of the **city** tumbled down!

cloud

A **cloud** is made of tiny drops of water. **Clouds** float high up in the sky. God gave his people a **cloud** to follow. It led them to the special land.

coat

A **coat** is a loose-fitting robe. Jacob gave his favorite **son**, Joseph, a special **coat** that was brightly colored.

coin

A **coin** is a small piece of metal used as **money**. Peter caught a **fish** with a **coin** in its mouth!

colt

A **colt** is a young horse or donkey. Jesus sent two of his **disciples** to **find** a **colt** for him to ride.

covenant

A **covenant** is a **promise**. God made a **covenant** with Abraham. He promised to give Abraham more children than there are **stars** in the sky!

Cc

create

When you **create** something you make something out of nothing. God **created** the **world** in six days!

cross

A **cross** is two pieces of wood joined together. Jesus died for us on a **cross**.

crown

A **crown** is special band you wear on your head. **Kings** wear **crowns** to show they are **rulers**.

cubit

A **cubit** is a measurement used in **Bible** times. A **cubit** is the distance from a man's elbow to his fingertips. Noah's **ark** was 300 **cubits** long!

curse

A **curse** is the opposite of a **blessing**. To **curse** someone means you wish something bad would happen to them.

Dd

death

Death is the end of our lives here in this **world**. Jesus showed he was **stronger** than **death** when he made Lazarus **alive** again!

demon

A **demon** is a bad **spirit** from the **devil**. A group of **demons** entered some pigs and made them jump off a cliff. But Jesus is greater than **demons**.

den

A **den** is a **cave** or a hole in the ground where wild animals live. Daniel was thrown into a **lions' den**, but God kept him safe.

descendants

Your children, grandchildren, and great-grandchildren are your **descendants.** Abraham had more **descendants** than there are **stars** in the sky!

desert

A **desert** is a place where people do not live because it is too hot and dry. Moses and God's people wandered in the **desert** for 40 years!

devil

The **devil** is a bad **spirit** who is God's **enemy**. The **devil** looked like a **snake** when he tricked Eve into **disobeying**.

disciple

A **disciple** is someone who follows and learns from a special **teacher**. Jesus' **disciples believed** and **obeyed** him.

disobey

When you **disobey**, you don't do what someone asks you to do. Daniel's **friends disobeyed** the **king**.

dove

A **dove** is a small white bird. Noah sent a **dove** out to see if the **flood** was over.

dream

A **dream** is what happens in your mind when you are asleep. Joseph **dreamed** that the **stars**, sun and moon bowed down to him.

dumb

In the **Bible, dumb** doesn't mean silly or stupid. A **dumb** person is someone who can't talk. Jesus **healed dumb** people so they could talk.

Ee

eagle

An **eagle** is a big bird that can fly very fast. When a young **eagle** learns to fly, its mother catches it on her wings.

earthquake

An **earthquake** is when the ground shakes. God sent an **earthquake** to get Paul and Silas out of **prison**!

Egyptians

People who live in Egypt are called **Egyptians**. God's people were **slaves** to the **Egyptians** for a long time.

enemy

An **enemy** is someone who doesn't like you. Jesus told his **disciples** to **love** their **enemies**.

escape

If someone tries to catch you and you run away and hide, you **escape** from them. Paul **escaped** from the **Jews** in Damascus – in a **basket**!

eternal life

Eternal means forever. **Eternal life** is the **new** kind of **life** Jesus gives.

Ff

faith

Faith is **believing** that something is **true**. **Faith** is also believing in or **trusting** someone to tell the truth. Jesus told us to have **faith** in God.

family

A **family** is a group of people who are related to each other. **Families love** and **help** one another.

famine

A **famine** is when the food crops won't grow. People become very hungry because there is not enough food.

feast

A **feast** is a special meal and party. God's people had **feasts** to **worship** and thank God for looking after them.

find

If you look for something, you are trying to **find** it. Jesus told a story about a **shepherd** who **found** his **lost sheep**.

fire

Fire is the flame, heat and light that comes off when something burns. Moses heard God's voice coming from a bush on **fire** that didn't burn up!

first

First means before everything else. Adam and Eve were the **first** people.

fish

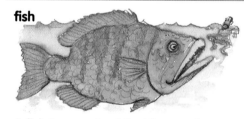

A **fish** is an animal that lives and breathes under water. Jonah was swallowed by a big **fish**.

fishermen

People who catch **fish** and **sell** them are called **fishermen**. Many of Jesus' friends were **fishermen**.

Ff

flock

A **flock** is a group of animals or birds. David was a **shepherd** who watched over a **flock** of **sheep**.

flood

A **flood** is when water covers the dry land. Once, God sent a **flood** to cover the earth. God kept Noah, his **family**, and the animals safe from the **flood**.

follower — see **disciple**

fool

A **fool** is someone who is silly and not smart. A **fool** doesn't understand what is important in **life**.

forget

If you don't remember something, you **forget** it.

forgive

When someone hurts you but you tell them it's OK, you **forgive** them. You don't try to get even. Joseph **forgave** his **brothers**.

frankincense

Frankincense is a very expensive **perfume**. One of the presents the **wise men** gave Jesus was **frankincense**.

free

1. If something is **free**, you do not have to pay anything to get it.

2. When you can do what you want, you are **free**. God sent Moses to **free** his people from the **Egyptians**.

friend

A **friend** is someone you like and want to be with. A **friend** likes you, too. Jesus called his **disciples** his **friends**.

frog

A **frog** is a little animal that lives near water. **Frogs** can hop and jump. God sent a **plague** of **frogs** to Egypt.

furnace

A **furnace** is a place made of brick or **stone** or metal that holds **fire**. God **saved** Shadrach, Meshach and Abednego from burning in a **furnace**.

Gg

Gentiles

People who were not God's **chosen** people were called **Gentiles**. After Jesus came, anyone could be part of God's people – even **Gentiles**!

giant

A **giant** is someone who is very tall and big. Goliath was a **giant** – he was over nine feet tall!

gift

A **gift** is a present you give to someone. When Jesus was born, **wise men** brought him **gifts**.

gleaning

Gleaning is picking up the leftover grain in the fields after **harvest**. Ruth gathered food by **gleaning** the fields.

glory

Glory is a sign of how great God is. When we **praise** God, that is called giving God **glory**.

gnat

A **gnat** is a small bug that can fly. God sent a **plague** of **gnats** to Egypt when **Pharaoh** wouldn't **free** God's people.

Gg

gold

Gold is a very expensive shiny yellow metal. The **wise men** gave Jesus **gold**.

golden calf

A **baby** cow is called a **calf**. God's people made a **calf** out of **gold** and **worshiped** it as if it were a god.

Gospel

Gospel means good news. The story of how Jesus died to **save** us is called the **Gospel** – it is good news!

grace

Grace is the **kindness** and **love** you give someone, even though they don't deserve it. We go to **Heaven** because of God's **grace**.

guard

When you **guard** something, you make sure nothing happens to it. **Roman soldiers guarded** Jesus' **tomb**.

guilt

Guilt means you've done wrong. Usually **guilt** makes you feel bad.

Hh

hallowed

Hallowed means **holy** or very special to God. In the Lord's **prayer**, we say "**Hallowed** be your name." That means God's name is special.

harp

A **harp** is a musical instrument with strings. David played the **harp** for Saul.

harvest

To **harvest** means you gather crops when they are ripe.

hate

When you really don't like something, you **hate** it. Jesus said we shouldn't **hate** other people – not even our **enemies**.

heal

If you make a sick person well, you **heal** them. Doctors use medicine to **heal** people. Jesus **healed** sick people. But he didn't use medicine!

heart

Your **heart** makes **blood** go around your **body**. Sometimes, people say your **heart** is the part that **loves** others.

Heaven

Heaven is where God is. **Heaven** is a very happy place. God's people will live in **Heaven** with him forever.

Hell

Hell is where the **devil** is. **Hell** is a place for anyone who **hates** God. God does not want anyone to go to **Hell**.

help

When you do something for someone, you **help** them. God **helped** his people **escape** from Egypt.

high priest

The **high priest** was the most important **priest**.

Hh Ii Jj

holy

To be **holy** means to be different and special. God is **holy** because he never does anything wrong.

honor

If you **honor** someone, you show them they are special. The **Bible** tells us to **honor** our mother and father.

hope

Hope is looking forward to something you are sure will happen. When you **hope** in God, you **believe** that God will make everything all right.

hosanna

Hosanna means "**save** us now!" In Jesus' time, it was a shout of great happiness.

humble

When you are **humble**, you don't brag about yourself. Moses was **humble**.

idol

An **idol** is a made-up god. In **Bible** times, some people **worshiped** and **prayed** to **idols** instead of to God.

incense

Incense is a **perfume** that smells good when it is burned. The **priests** in the **temple** burned **incense**.

inn

An **inn** is a place to stay when you are traveling. An **inn** is like a motel. Mary and Joseph couldn't **find** a room in an **inn** when Jesus was born.

Israelites

God's special **chosen** people were called the **Israelites**. The **Israelites** were **descendants** of Abraham's grandson, Jacob.

jealous

If you are **jealous**, you want something someone else has. King Saul was **jealous** of David because the people liked David best.

Jews

The **Jews** were God's **chosen** people in the **Old Testament**. Another name for the **Jews** is the **Israelites**.

joy

Joy is the deep happy feeling we get from **knowing** that God **loves** us.

judge

A **judge** decides who is right when there is a quarrel. **Judges helped** Moses look after God's people.

justice

Justice is what is fair and right. A **judge** wants to give people **justice**.

Kk   Ll

kind

A **kind** person is someone who **helps** and **loves** other people. Jesus said we should be **kind** to each other.

king

A **king** is the leader of a country or a people. Joash was a **king** at seven!

kingdom

A **kingdom** is all the land and people that a **king** rules over. **Christians** are part of God's **kingdom**.

kiss

When you **kiss** someone, you touch them with your lips. You **kiss** people you like or **love**.

kneel

When you **kneel**, you get down on your knees. People **kneel** before a **king**, and sometimes people **kneel** to **pray**.

know

To **know** something means you understand it and you are sure about it.

lamb

A **lamb** is a young **sheep**. The **Jews** used to **sacrifice lambs** to say they were sorry for their **sins**.

lame

A person who is **lame** cannot walk. Paul **healed** a **lame** man.

Last Supper

The last meal Jesus ate with his **disciples** was called the **Last Supper**.

law

A **law** is a rule to follow. God's **laws** are called the **Ten Commandments**.

leprosy

Leprosy is a bad skin disease. Most people don't want to go near **lepers** in case they catch **leprosy**. Jesus liked people no one else did – even **lepers**.

letter

A **letter** is a written message you send to someone. Parts of the **Bible** are **letters**. Paul wrote **letters** to **churches** and to some of his **friends**.

liar

A **liar** is someone who doesn't say what is **true**. Joseph's **brothers** were **liars** when they told their father that Joseph was dead.

lie

A **lie** is something that is not **true**. The **Bible** says we should not tell **lies**.

life

Life is the **power** inside you that makes you **alive**. Jesus brought Lazarus back to **life**.

lion

A **lion** is a big wild cat. The **king** of Babylon put Daniel in a **den** of **lions**.

Ll

locust

A **locust** is a bug that looks like a grasshopper. God sent **locusts** to Egypt, and they ate all the plants.

lord

Lord is another word for **king** or master. Jesus is called the **Lord** because he is the King of all the kings.

lost

When you can't **find** something, it is **lost**. Jesus told a story about a woman who searched for her **lost coin**.

lots

Lots were sticks or **stones** or bones. People threw **lots**, like dice, to **help** them to decide about something.

love

To **love** means to like something or someone very much. **Love** means caring. God **loves** each of us.

Mm

magi — see **wise men**

magic

Tricks that seem like **miracles** but really aren't are called **magic**. Pharaoh's magicians did **magic** tricks for Moses.

manger

A **manger** is a feeding box for animals. Mary laid Jesus in a **manger**.

manna

The special food God gave the **Israelites** in the **desert** was called **manna**. It means, "What is it?"

mercy

When you have **mercy**, you give people another chance to do good when they have messed up. God has **mercy** on us.

Messiah

The word **Messiah** means the one God **chose**. Jesus is the **Messiah**.

miracle

A **miracle** is a wonderful thing that only God can do. **Miracles** show us how **powerful** God is.

money

Money is something people use to buy things with. In **Bible** times, **money** was usually pieces of metal, like silver or **gold** coins.

money changers

Money changers were people who swapped **money** from one country for money from another country. Many **money changers** tried to cheat people.

mourning

When people are very sad because they have **lost** something or a **friend** has died, they are **mourning**.

myrrh

Myrrh was an expensive **perfume** and pain killer. **Myrrh** was one of Jesus' birthday presents from the **wise men**!

Nn

nail

A **nail** is a sharp pointy piece of metal. A carpenter uses **nails** to fasten pieces of wood together.

neighbor

Hi! We've just moved here.

Mom! The new neighbors are here!

A **neighbor** is someone who lives near you. Jesus said everyone we meet is our **neighbor** and we should **love** them.

net

Close one!

A **net** is a lot of strings tied together to hold something. **Fishermen** catch **fish** by throwing a **net** into the water.

new

Wow! what's that?

Well, it's new!

When something is **new**, it has never been seen or used or tried out before. When people become **Christians**, they have a **new life**.

New Testament

Malachi Ch.4
Ch.3

THE NEW TESTAMENT
MATTHEW
ch.1

The **New Testament** is the second part of the **Bible**. The **New Testament** tells about Jesus, the **church** and God's **new covenant** with his people.

Oo

oath — see **vow**

obey

Shechem

Ur 20m

If you **obey** someone, you do what they tell you to do. Abraham **obeyed** God and left his home.

ointment — see **perfume**

old

When I was your age, Adam was still alive!

Someone or something that is **old** has been around a long time. Methuselah lived to be 969 years **old**!

Old Testament

THE OLD TESTAMENT
GENESIS
ch.1

The **Old Testament** is the **first** part of the **Bible**. The **Old Testament** tells of God's people and **law** before Jesus.

ox

An **ox** is a big, **strong** animal that looks like a cow. When you have more than one **ox**, you call them **oxen**. **Oxen** were used to pull carts and plows.

Pp

palace

They started building before you were born!

A **palace** is a very big house where a **king** or **queen** lives. King Solomon took 13 years to build his **palace**!

palm trees

Palm trees grow in hot countries. When Jesus rode to Jerusalem, people waved branches from **palm trees**.

parable

There was a man who had two sons...

A **parable** is a story that **teaches** something. Jesus told many **parables**.

paradise — see **Heaven**

Passover

Yuk!

Bitter herbs! They're what we ate when we were in Egypt.

The **Passover** is a Jewish **feast** day. At **Passover**, **Jews** remember when God **freed** them from being **slaves** in Egypt.

patience

They're almost ready to pick.

We can wait a little longer.

When you have **patience**, you wait calmly and without complaining. **Patience** means you can wait a long time, even when things go wrong.

Pp

peace

Peace is when you feel happy and **know** things are OK. **Peace** is getting along with others and not fighting.

pearl

A **pearl** is a very expensive round bead used in jewelry. Jesus said that his **kingdom** is precious, like a **pearl** that a man **sells** everything to buy.

perfume

Perfume is an expensive liquid that smells nice. Mary washed Jesus' feet with **perfume**.

pharaoh

The **king** of Egypt was called the **pharaoh**. **Pharaoh** got so tired of the **plagues**, he let the **Israelites** go.

Pharisees

The **Pharisees** were **Jews** who made sure the Jewish **laws** were kept. The **Pharisees** didn't like Jesus because he **loved** people more than laws.

Philistines

The **Philistines** were **enemies** of God's people. Goliath was a **Philistine**.

pillar

A **pillar** is a big pole of wood or **stone** that holds up a roof. Samson knocked down the **pillars** of an **enemy temple**.

plague

A **plague** is a very bad thing that happens to a group of people. God sent ten **plagues** on the **Egyptians**. He wanted his people to go **free**.

potter

Someone who makes pots out of clay is called a **potter**. God said he is like a **potter**, and we are like the clay.

power

When you are **strong** and you can do things, you have **power**. Jesus gave his **apostles** **power** to **heal** the sick and to get rid of **demons**.

praise

When you say that someone is great and wonderful and good, you are **praising** them. We **praise** God.

pray

1. When we talk to God, we **pray**.

2. What you say when you **pray** is called a **prayer**. Jesus **taught** us the **Lord's Prayer**.

preach

To **preach** means to tell people the good news about God and Jesus. Paul **preached** in many lands.

priest

A **priest** was someone in charge of **worship**. A **priest** offered **sacrifices**.

prison

A **prison** is like a cage. People who break the **law** are kept in **prison**. Many **Christians** were put in **prison** for **believing** in Jesus.

Pp

promise

When you **promise** to do something, you are saying you will do it no matter what. God **promised** Noah he would never **flood** the whole earth again.

prophet

A **prophet** was a messenger who spoke for God. A **prophet** told people what was going to happen and what God wanted them to do.

proud

People who are **proud** think they are better than everyone else. God doesn't want us to be **proud**.

proverb

A short saying that is **true** and full of **wisdom** is called a **proverb**. Solomon wrote many **proverbs**.

psalm

A **psalm** is a song. The book of **Psalms** is like a songbook. King David wrote many **psalms**.

punish

When you do something wrong, you are **punished**.

Qq

quail

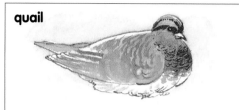

A **quail** is a small bird that is good to eat. God sent **quail** for his people to eat when they were in the **desert**.

queen

A **queen** is a woman who **rules** over a country. Esther became a **queen** in Persia and **saved** her people.

Rr

rabbi

Rabbi means **teacher**. Jesus' **disciples** called him **rabbi**.

rain

Rain is water that falls from **clouds** in the sky. Once, God made it **rain** so much that all the earth was **flooded**.

rainbow

A **rainbow** is an arch of seven colors in the sky. You see a **rainbow** when the sun comes out after it **rains**. After the **flood**, God made a **rainbow** for Noah.

redeem

To **redeem** means to buy something back. In the **Bible**, **redeem** also meant to pay the price to **free** a **slave**.

reeds

Reeds are tall grasses that grow along the edge of ponds, lakes and rivers. **Pharaoh's** daughter found **baby** Moses in the **reeds** by the Nile River.

rejoice

To **rejoice** means to be very happy. **Rejoicing** is like having a party! Jesus wants us to **rejoice** – God **loves** us.

repent

When you **repent**, you are sorry for doing something wrong and you don't do it again. John the Baptist told people to **repent**.

resurrection

Resurrection is when a **dead** person comes back to **life**. Jesus' **resurrection** means we can live in **Heaven** forever!

Rr

rich

If you are **rich**, you have a lot of **money**. Jesus said it's hard for a **rich** person to get into **Heaven**.

righteousness

Righteousness means being close to God and doing what is right. God **saved** Noah from the **flood** because Noah was **righteous**.

rod

A **rod** is a stick or a club. God turned Moses' **rod** into a **snake** to show **Pharaoh** how much **power** he had.

Romans

The **Romans** were **rulers** over the **Jews** at the time of Jesus.

ruler

A **ruler** is someone who leads others and tells them what to do. **Pharaoh** was the **ruler** of Egypt.

Ss

sabbath

The **sabbath** is the seventh day of the week. The **sabbath** was a special day.

sacrifice

A **sacrifice** is something special you give up. God's people **sacrificed** their special animals to God to show they were sorry for their **sins**.

Samaritan

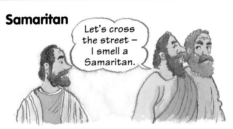

A **Samaritan** was someone who lived in Samaria. **Jews** and **Samaritans** did not like each other.

sandals

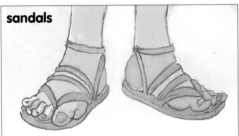

Sandals were the shoes worn in **Bible** times. Moses had to take off his **sandals** to go near the burning bush.

Sanhedrin

The **Sanhedrin** was the most important **Jewish** court. Stephen's trial was held in front of the **Sanhedrin**.

Satan — see **devil**

save

To **save** someone means to keep bad things from happening to them. Jesus **saves** us from our **sins**.

savior

A **savior** is someone who **saves** people from danger. The name "Jesus" means **savior**. Jesus is our **Savior**.

scribe

Someone who wrote out copies of the **Scriptures** was called a **scribe**. Some **scribes taught** the Scriptures to others.

Scriptures — see **Bible**

seed

A **seed** is what you plant to grow something. Jesus said God's **kingdom** is like a big tree that grows from only a tiny **seed**.

sell

If someone **sells** you something, they give it to you and you give them something else for it.

serve

When you **serve** someone, you do something to **help** them. Jesus **served** his **friends** by washing their feet.

share

When you give part of what you have to someone, you **share** it. In **New Testament** times, **Christians shared** everything they had.

sheep

A **sheep** is an animal with a thick woolly coat. **Sheep** need someone to look after them and lead them. David looked after his father's **sheep**.

shepherd

A **shepherd** is someone who looks after **sheep**. A **shepherd** keeps the sheep safe. Jesus cares for us like a **shepherd** cares for his sheep.

shield

A **shield** is a piece of metal or wood that **soldiers** held in **battle**. The **shield** kept the soldier from getting hurt.

ships

Ships are big boats that can sail on the sea or the ocean. Jonah tried to run away from God by **escaping** on a **ship**.

sin

When we **sin**, we do, say or think something that is wrong. **Sin** hurts God. We **sin** when we are unkind.

slave

A **slave** was someone owned by someone else, just like a car or a house is owned by someone. God's people were **slaves** to the **Egyptians**.

sling

A **sling** is a weapon used for throwing rocks. David only had a **sling** and five **stones** when he beat Goliath.

snake

A **snake** is a long, slithery animal with no legs. When God told Moses to throw down his **rod**, it turned into a **snake**.

soldier

A person who is in the **army** is a **soldier**. A **Roman soldier** asked Jesus to **heal** his servant – and Jesus did!

son

A little boy is his parents' **son**. Jacob had 12 boys, so he had 12 **sons**.

soul

Your **soul** is your inside part that makes you **alive**. When God breathed **life** into Adam, he became a living **soul**.

sower

A **sower** is a farmer. Jesus' story of the **sower** is about a farmer planting **seed**.

sparrow

A **sparrow** is a little brown bird. God **knows** and cares about everything, even the smallest **sparrow**!

spirit

Your **spirit** is the part inside of you that makes you who you are. You can't see your **spirit**, but it lives forever.

stable

A **stable** is a building or **cave** where farm animals are kept. Jesus was born in a **stable**.

Ss   Tt

staff

A **shepherd's** walking stick is called a **staff**. Shepherds also use a **staff** to keep their **sheep** out of trouble.

star

The tiny lights you see in the sky at night are called **stars**. The **wise men** followed a special **star** to Jesus.

stone

A **stone** is a small rock. David beat Goliath with just one **stone**!

strong

Someone who is **strong** can do things that are hard to do, like lifting very heavy things. Samson was very **strong**.

synagogue

The **Jews** met together in buildings called **synagogues**. They met in a **synagogue** to read and learn about the **Scriptures**.

tabernacle

The **tabernacle** was a meeting **tent**. When the **Jews** were in the **desert** they **worshiped** in the **tabernacle**.

talent

A **talent** was used to measure how much **money** you had. Jesus told a story about a man who gave **talents** to his servants.

tax

A **tax** is **money** that has to be paid to the government. People paid their **taxes** to a **tax** collector. **Tax** collectors often cheated people.

teach

When someone **teaches** you, they **help** you learn something. Jesus and his **disciples taught** about God's **love**.

temple

A **temple** is a special building to **worship** God in. Solomon built a great **temple** in Jerusalem.

temptation

Temptation is when we think something looks all right to do, but it would really hurt us.

Ten Commandments

A **commandment** is a rule to follow. The **Ten Commandments** were the rules God gave Moses.

tent

A **tent** is a shelter. **Tents** were made of skins or cloth and held up by ropes and poles. Paul made **tents**.

throne

A **throne** is a big, beautiful chair for a **king** or **queen**. King Solomon had a **throne** covered with **gold** and it had six steps going up to it.

tithe

A **tithe** means a tenth. The **Jews** gave a tenth of what they earned to God.

Tt

tomb

A place where dead people are **buried** is called a **tomb**. Jesus' **friends** found his **tomb** empty!

tower

A **tower** is a very tall, narrow building. Once, some people tried to build a **tower** tall enough to reach to **Heaven**. It was called the **Tower** of Babel.

town

A **town** is a place where people live that is smaller than a **city**. Jesus was born in the **town** of Bethlehem.

tribe

A **tribe** was a **family** group. One man's **descendants** made a **tribe**.

true

When something is **true**, it is real and right. It is not false or wrong. Elijah proved God was the **true** God when God sent **fire** to light his **sacrifice**.

trumpet

A **trumpet** is an instrument you blow air through to make a loud noise. God's people blew their **trumpets** and God made the walls of Jericho fall down!

trust

When you **trust** someone, you **believe** everything they tell you. You know they would never do anything to hurt you.

twins

Twins are two **babies** born at the same time from the same mother. Jacob and Esau were **twins**.

Uu

unclean

When something is **unclean**, it is dirty and it is not good for you. **Jews** thought some food was **unclean**.

unleavened bread

Unleavened bread is **bread** that doesn't have any **yeast**. It is flat and hard like a cracker.

upper room

An **upper room** is a room on the roof of a house. Jesus and his **disciples** ate the **Last Supper** in a big **upper room**.

Vv

veil

A piece of material to cover your head and face is called a **veil**. Rebekah wore a **veil** when she met Isaac.

vine

A **vine** is a plant that has a long stem and grapes grow on it. A **vine** grows up fences or along the ground.

vineyard

A **vineyard** is where lots of **vines** grow.

vision

A **vision** was like a **dream** you had when you were awake or asleep. God used **visions** to tell people what to do or what would happen.

vow

A **vow** is a very serious **promise**. Nazirites were men who **vowed** never to do certain things – including not to cut their hair!

watchman

A **watchman** is a **guard**. **Watchmen** stood on **city** walls to watch out for danger. Or they guarded crops in the fields at **harvest**.

wedding

A **wedding** is a special time when a man and a woman get married. Jesus went to a **wedding** in Cana.

weep

Weep is another word for cry. People **weep** when they are sad. Jesus **wept** at the **tomb** of his **friend** Lazarus.

well

Well?

I'm Rebekah.

A **well** is a deep hole dug in the ground that holds water. Abraham's servant **found** Rebekah by a **well**.

widow

Lord, this is all I have.

A **widow** is a woman whose husband has died. A poor **widow** in the **temple** gave her last two **coins**.

wind

When there is a **wind**, the air moves. **Wind** is what makes a kite fly and what blows leaves off a tree. Once, Jesus made a scary **wind** stop blowing.

wine

Wine is a special drink made from grapes. People made **wine** by pressing grapes – with their feet!

wisdom

One bit of wisdom – when you're not sure about something, ask, "What would the Lord do?"

When you have **wisdom**, you understand what is really important in **life**. This **wisdom** is from God.

wise men

Men who studied the **stars** were called **wise men**. Some **wise men** from the east followed a star to Jesus.

witness

You knew Jesus?

Yes! Let me tell you what I know!

If you are a **witness**, you say what you have seen or what you **know**. Jesus' **disciples** were **witnesses** for him.

word

Thus saith the Lord...

In the **Bible**, **word** means God's message to us. The **Word** of God is all the things God wants to say to us. The Bible is the **Word** of God.

world

The **world** is another name for the earth. Sometimes **world** also means all the people on the earth. God made the **world** and everything in it!

worship

My soul glorifies the Lord, and my spirit rejoices in God my savior.

To **worship** someone means you thank them and **praise** them as God. We **worship** God because he deserves it.

yeast

WITHOUT

WITH

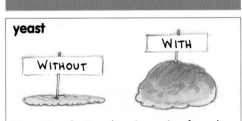

Yeast is what makes **bread** soft and fluffy. God's people left Egypt in such a hurry, they had to take their bread without any **yeast** in it.

yoke

A **yoke** is a wooden bar that goes over the necks of two animals so that they can pull together.